Get Locked-In

Mastering the Art of Laser Focus to Achieve Your Dreams

#1 Best Selling Author

Kelly Cole

Published By: Publishing Advantage Group
www.PublishingAdvantageGroup.com

For ordering, booking, permission, questions, or interviews, contact
info@primetime-marketing.com.

Printed in the United States of America

First Printing 2017

Cover Design: Fernando Palacios (I AM A SOLUTION CONSULTING FIRM, LLC)

Cover Photography: Nazareth's Photography @NazarethsPhotography

ISBN: 978-1983414220
ISBN-13: 978-1983414220

FORWARD

Everybody wants to talk and very few people if any, listen. People talk a good game but, very few accomplish anything. Setting goals is simple. All you have to do is write them down on a piece of paper or share them with another person. I've found that some of the most successful people listen and follow the instructions of someone that has already paved the way. Would you believe me if I told you Kelly Cole is a great listener, probably not because you don't know me? You have purchased his book, that was the easy part. Now you have to put in the work and apply the principles he's laid out for you to achieve success. Our society has many phases that are a part of our everyday dialog like, "The proof was in the pudding" and Trust the Process. It's easy to say these things and the world is embracing the logic behind the phase because saying it easier than doing it. At the end of the day, you'll have to be accountable for the words that come out of your mouth. What's the point to all this, simple, trust those who've already run the race you are embarking on. Trust is very important and the person that wrote this book is leaving no stone unturned. I can say without a doubt that this author has listened, applied the principles that he was taught and experienced the journey for himself. The book is just information that is being passed down, the key is how you apply it to find or define your success.

Kelly has some of the best adjectives to define a man, work ethic, fearless, driven and the courage to dream big. This book is a roadmap but you'll have to drive forward to achieve your own goals. Failure comes from not today, I'll do it tomorrow. Tomorrow is not promised and all we have is this moment. Nothing is given, and everything is earned, that way you'll always appreciate every step of your experience. Get up every day and move forward to your success. Stop allowing other people to derail you from your greatness. This book is the blueprint and is filled with facts that will benefit the reader.

Belief in yourself will set the stage, you are an actor and this book is your script. Every good actor learns his or her lines until that performance looks effortless. This is your guide and you'll have to study it in order for your appearance to bridge the gap which will propel you to your destiny. Let page one be the first step toward the life you've always dreamed about. Believe, Receive and Achieve...

Rodney Johnson

Professional Comedian for Over 30yrs, He has been seen on Oprah with Sinbad, HBO, BET Comic View, Parent Hood with Robert Townsend, Hit TV Show Thea, VH1 with Rosie O'Donnell.

CONTENTS

INTRODUCTION

HOW DO I THINK?

My coaching client asked, "How do you think?" I had to stop and think about it for a second. How do I think? What experiences have I had in my life that have shaped the way that I think? Am I too focused? Do I work too hard? Am I too serious? Am I chasing money? Why do I work so hard?

All of these questions run through my mind daily as I share my thoughts with people. I can tell by their reactions that they think I'm lost or even crazy for that matter, because of my intense focus to achieve what I desire out of life.

So, what do I think? I think that if a man doesn't work, he doesn't eat. I think every second of my day should be used, not one second should be wasted. I think that the reason most people don't achieve what they want out of life is because they lack focus, a clear-cut goal, and a plan to get there. I think a lot of people would rather party than grind. I feel like if I'm going to party I want to have something to celebrate. Why are you partying if you haven't accomplished anything? I think most people would rather take a shortcut than actually put in the work to achieve what they want out of life. I think too many people would rather make excuses than to make it happen.

I believe literally coming from nothing has given me an advantage. It has created a drive and will to succeed that I really can't describe. Growing up it hurt not having the fly clothes and sneakers like the cool kids. I felt left out. I always said, "My kids would never feel that pain." Therefore, it has been my quest to provide the life I never had for them.

I was born in the most notorious housing project in the world, "Cabrini Green" in Chicago, IL. Most people know it as the place where the TV show *Good Times*, and movies such as *Coolie High*, *Hoop Dreams*, and *Candyman* were filmed. I was raised on food stamps and government cheese with the rats and the roaches. Don't get me wrong my mom and dad they everything they could to make sure I was fed, clothed, and safe in the mean streets of Chicago. A lot of the time, I think about the little things my mom did to make me feel special. I think about things like how she would make my oatmeal with butter and brown sugar in the mornings before she took me to school. It made me feel so special because of how much love she put into every meal she made for me and my sister.

My mom and dad never married, so I have maybe one or two memories of us all living in the same house. Even with that being the case, I must admit, my dad has always been in my life as far back as I can remember. To be completely honest a lot of the great qualities I have come from him. I've never met anyone who worked as hard as my dad and has a no-quit-balls-out attitude about everything he does. Growing up, I wanted to be just like my dad, he is a master salesman. At one point he sold vacuum cleaners door to door and made a lot of money doing so. One day, he came home and told me he sold a vacuum cleaner for $1,000 to a guy that didn't even have any carpet. I just stood there in amazement.

Back to my point, my parents did everything in their power to provide for every need that I had growing up. I learned quickly that if I wanted to wear Jordans and the designer clothes all the other kids were wearing, I had to go out and get it on my own. So, believe it or not, I started my first business at age six with my best friend, my sister Kandice. We call her Keke. Keke and I carried her little table and chairs down to the front of our building. We grabbed every piece of candy we could find in the house and opened a candy store. The funny thing is people stopped and bought candy from us. They would ask, "How much is your candy?" We would reply "Quarter, Nickle, Dime, whatever you want to pay for it!" I can't help but laugh when I think about that. We had no clue what we were doing, but we had an idea to start a candy store. We got off our butts and actually did it. That is more than a lot of adults I know, that have great ideas and haven't done anything because of fear.

What are 3 things I know to be true about life?

1) Laser Focused Hard Work Pays Off!

2) There Are No Shortcuts to Success!

3) Your Dreams Don't Care How You Feel!

What motivates me? What is my why?

My kids are my motivation. I have three of the smartest, beautiful, and talented kids on the planet. My son Aaron is the oldest (18), then there is my daughter Alexis (16) and my baby girl Alove (12). I work hard to provide them the life I didn't have growing up.

You need to get the drive of a person who comes from nothing.

When you come from nothing your will and drive to succeed is on a whole other level. You develop a hunger that can only be quenched by success or having more than enough. You should want more not just for you, you should want more to take care of your family. If your mom is still working that should be your fuel. If your grandma is still working that should be fuel. If anyone in your family is struggling to make ends meet that should be fuel. My goal is to give away a million dollars. I want to give 100 people $10,000 dollars. I've had this dream for over 10 years. When I worked at Walmart I used to think about it every day. I would write the numbers 1 to 100 and write the names of people I wanted to bless with $10,000. If you are only thinking about yourself when it comes to why you do or don't want to be successful, check your heart because that's selfish.

Every morning I wake up 6 a.m. What gets me out of bed is knowing that my babies are counting on me, they may need something today or my mom may call and need something. I realized a long time ago it's not about me, it's about who is depending on me to make it happen and who I can serve.

My mentor told me once, "Kelly, only women, and children are allowed to make excuses, men make it happen!" I never forgot that quote. So, every day I wake up my goal is to make it happen, whatever it is. For me, it is providing for my family and working toward my goals.

Comfort Is the Enemy Of Success!

What Do You Want to Accomplish This Year?

In the space provided below write it down.

_____

_____

_____

_____

_____

_____

_____

_____

_____

_____

_____

_____

_____

_____

_____

_____

_____

_____

_____

_____

_____

_____

_____

_____

_____

_____

_____

_____

_____

_____

_____

_____

_____

_____

_____

CHAPTER 1

LOOK

WHAT ARE YOU LOOKING AT?

It's very important that you visualize and meditate on what you want to accomplish. Write your goals down and put them before your eyes daily. Read them in the morning before you start your day and at night before you go to sleep.

Be careful what you look at. Believe it or not, you produce what you see! Mike Murdock was quoted as saying, "Don't put anything in front of you, that you don't want in you!" Think about it, if you watch enough McDonald's commercials you are going to want a Big Mac. I would bet money that just by you reading the words Big Mac you got a picture of one in your head. Even if you don't go out and get one, one day the image will still come to your mind, you may even get a craving for one.

One of my favorite stories in the bible is Genesis 30:25-31:16 it backs my point, stick with me.

²⁵ And it came to pass, when Rachel had born Joseph, that Jacob said unto Laban, Send me away, that I may go unto mine own place, and to my country.

²⁶ Give me my wives and my children, for whom I have served thee, and let me go: for thou knowest my service which I have done thee.

[27] And Laban said unto him, I pray thee, if I have found favour in thine eyes, tarry: for I have learned by experience that the Lord hath blessed me for thy sake.

[28] And he said, Appoint me thy wages, and I will give it.

[29] And he said unto him, Thou knowest how I have served thee, and how thy cattle was with me.

[30] For it was little which thou hadst before I came, and it is now increased unto a multitude, and the Lord hath blessed thee since my coming: and now when shall I provide for mine own house also?

[31] And he said, What shall I give thee? And Jacob said, Thou shalt not give me anything: if thou wilt do this thing for me, I will again feed and keep thy flock.

[32] I will pass through all thy flock to day, removing from thence all the speckled and spotted cattle, and all the brown cattle among the sheep, and the spotted and speckled among the goats: and of such shall be my hire.

[33] So shall my righteousness answer for me in time to come, when it shall come for my hire before thy face: every one that is not speckled and spotted among the goats, and brown among the sheep, that shall be counted stolen with me.

[34] And Laban said, Behold, I would it might be according to thy word.

[35] And he removed that day the he goats that were ringstraked and spotted, and all the she goats that were

speckled and spotted, and every one that had some white in it, and all the brown among the sheep, and gave them into the hand of his sons.

[36] And he set three days' journey betwixt himself and Jacob: and Jacob fed the rest of Laban's flocks.

[37] And Jacob took him rods of green poplar, and of the hazel and chestnut tree, and pilled white strakes in them, and made the white appear which was in the rods.

[38] And he set the rods which he had pilled before the flocks in the gutters in the watering troughs when the flocks came to drink, that they should conceive when they came to drink.

[39] And the flocks conceived before the rods, and brought forth cattle ringstraked, speckled, and spotted.

[40] And Jacob did separate the lambs, and set the faces of the flocks toward the ringstraked, and all the brown in the flock of Laban; and he put his own flocks by themselves, and put them not unto Laban's cattle.

[41] And it came to pass, whensoever the stronger cattle did conceive, that Jacob laid the rods before the eyes of the cattle in the gutters, that they might conceive among the rods.

[42] But when the cattle were feeble, he put them not in: so the feebler were Laban's, and the stronger Jacob's.

[43] And the man increased exceedingly, and had much cattle, and maidservants, and menservants, and camels, and

asses.

What Did Jacob Do?

Did you see it in verses 37-39? Jacob took the rods of green poplar and pilled white strakes in them, and made the white which was in the rods appear.

Next, he set the peeled rods before the flocks in the gutters and in the watering troughs. When the flocks came to drink, they should conceive.

Jacob put rods with spots in front of the calves when they drank and mated, The calves produced what they saw! WOW!

Verse 39 "And the flocks conceived before the rods, and brought forth cattle ringstraked, speckled, and spotted."

Now you mean to tell me, as a living, breathing, man or woman you can't do the same thing by placing before your eyes daily what you want to produce and give birth to in your life?

If you are not where you want to be in life ask yourself, what have I been looking at? Some of the things that are in our lives are not there because we chose to put them there. They are there because someone else placed them in front of us such as our parents, family, or friends. You may need to change your environment. You may need to change the group of people you hang with, some of them may even be family members. Just be prepared for the people in your life who call you crazy, stuck-up, or tell you that you are full of yourself because are choosing to take control of your life and go after the things you want. It's not selfish to work on you. Whoever doesn't get it or respect and encourage your growth, choose to love them from afar and get locked-in on what you want out of your life.

If you want to take it a step further, you have a responsibility to be something that the next generation will want and need to look up to. Be someone that you would want your kids to model and reproduce.

WINNERS
—— focus on ——
WINNING

THE POWER OF VISUALIZATION
AND REPETITION

I remember playing football my freshman year in Chicago at Weber High school, by the way, which was the same high school that Mike Krzyzewski aka Coach K, head coach of the Duke Blue-devils attended. At the start season, we were so excited and had high hopes of having a great season. We came out and lost our first three games, I was so upset and told the coach, "I'm quitting!" I remember the exact play I made up in my mind. I was quitting. Our cornerback had just got burnt down the sideline on a 60-yard bomb pass, as I'm watching the guy run down the sideline heading toward the end-zone, I just walked off the field. I could not go through a whole season of not winning one game like I did all my previous years of playing pee wee & midget football. I told the coach, "I'm done!"

My coach told me, "Cole, do not quit this team!"

I said, "Coach I'm Done! I Quit!"

He said, "Cole, do not quit! If we win all of the rest of our games, we have a great chance to be the district champions and all I'm asking you to do is not give up on me and the team."

I said, "OK I won't quit, but we better turn this thing around A.S.A.P. or I'm out!"

After the game Coach told us all to take a seat and pay attention to the chalkboard. He wrote down a list of our last seven games, which happened to be the toughest teams in the district! He told us all he wanted us to do is take it one game at a time and commit to giving our all every single play. He said, "I want you to promise me you are going to play every play as if it was your last! I want you to never give up! Can you all make that promise to me?" Everyone agreed.

The next day at practice my coach walks up to me and hands me a bag, I said: "What's this?"

He said, "Just open it, I got you something." I opened it and it was a pair of black leather lineman gloves. I loved those gloves, I kept them my whole high school career. They even began the tear by my senior year, I just taped them up and kept playing. They made me feel invisible. That day at practice, to my surprise everyone came with a new attitude and we were focused. We worked harder than we had ever worked to get prepared for our next game.

Believe it or not, we started winning. I thought to myself, "Okay, this thing is working." We were beating the best teams in the district. The coach got the whole team to believe in the goal. He promised us if we took it one game at a time and played at the level we were capable of, we would win the district championship!

The hardest game of the winning streak was the fifth game. It was against our crosstown rival Loyola High School. They were big, strong, and fast. The had a running back that was so fast and strong if we didn't hit him low, we were guaranteed to get run over. He was built like Mike Tyson but shorter and faster. That kid could run and hit hard. Their linemen were just as strong and fast. Running into those guys felt like hitting a brick wall. That game was so tough for us, but we pulled together and won. It wasn't a pretty win, but we got the victory and were one step closer to our goal. Our coach did a great job at keeping us focused. He made sure we were all on the same page and taking it one game at a time.

To achieve any goal or task it's important for you to know that you must envision it first in order to bring it to pass. Also, how you practice will become a habit. If you are slack in preparing for whatever it is that you want, it will not come to pass. Now, my dream that year was to score a touchdown in a game. As an offensive and defensive lineman there was no way they were going to give me the ball, so I knew if I was gonna score a touchdown I had to take the ball on defense and run it back for a touchdown. So before every game, I would practice this play. I was the defensive end; the running back was going to run the ball to my side and I was going to hit him, and he is going to drop the ball and I'm going to pick it up and run it back for the touchdown. Next, I was going to flip in the end-zone and do my dance. So, before every game, I would practice this same play over and over. I practiced so much that my teammates and coaches would ask me what I was doing. I'd say, "This what is going to happen! The running back is going to come around my side running the ball, I'm going to hit him, he's going to drop the ball and I'm going to run it back for a touchdown. Then I'm going to flip in the end-zone and I'm going to do my dance!" They laughed and said, "You're was crazy!"

Game after game went by and it didn't happen, but we kept on winning, so I was happy. Still, before every game, I would practice this: He's going to come around, I'm going to hit him, he's going to drop the ball and I'm going to run it back for a touchdown, then I'm going to flip in the end-zone and I'm going to do my dance.

The very last game of the year, the district championship game. Fourth quarter. The running back came running around to my side. I said, Awe, this is it!" It was just like I envisioned it! He came running to my side, I hit him, and he dropped the ball. I ran it back for a 70-yard touchdown! I flipped in the end-zone and did my dance. My teammates and coaches were on the sideline crying. They cried because what I envisioned, I manifested. They saw it come to pass and it brought tears to their eyes. We even got a penalty for my celebration dance, but we didn't care. We won the district championship after losing our first three games of the season! We were so happy, we were jumping around and screaming, "Number 1! Number 1 Baby! We did it! We did it!" We couldn't wait to dump the Gatorade cooler on our coach's head. As I'm writing this I'm laughing because I feel bad for coach, it was the dead of winter in Chicago and we dumped a large cooler of Gatorade on his head. I know that had to suck for him, he took it like a man I must say.

Chapter Points:

Be Careful What You Put Before Your Eyes

Be Careful What You Let Others Put Before Your Eyes

Only Put Before Your Eyes What You Want to Produce

You Produce What You See

It's Just as Important to Visualize What You Want, As It

Is to Look at It

Make a list below of at least 5 goals or dreams you want to manifest in your life:

1._____

2._____

3._____

4._____

5._____

_____

_____

_____

_____

_____

_____

_____

_____

In the Boxes Below Place a Picture of Something You Want to Manifest in Your Life

CHAPTER 2

OUTWORK
Work Harder, Faster, or Longer Than Everyone!

One of my favorite motivational speakers ET The Hip Hop Preacher said, "You may be smarter, you might come from privilege, your father might own a company, but you will not outwork me!"

You need to wake up with that attitude every day. Say It out loud, "I will not be outworked!" Some days you are going to have to work harder than you did the day before and you are going to have to move faster than you did the day before. Some days you are going to have to work longer than you ever have. When you get locked-in on your goal you are going to have to make up your mind that you are going to do whatever it takes to accomplish it.

Get things done faster! Even if you have to hire a couple of people to do somethings for you, get them done faster. The universe loves speed. Stop waiting for everything to be perfect before you take action! Done is always better done perfect! A millionaire changed my life with this one quote, he said: "You don't have to get it right, you just got to get it going!"

I remember the days when I first started my business. I didn't sleep! I always felt like I was going to miss an opportunity if I went to sleep. So many nights I worked until I just absolutely couldn't work any longer. Then I laid on the couch. I took a nap and got right back to work. I had things to do, I had to turn my dream into a reality. That meant I had to work longer than others.

19

DON'T STOP WORKING WHEN YOU ARE TIRED, STOP WHEN YOU ARE DONE!

I remember when I first quit my 2 jobs, I would literally pray every morning and night for God to bless my business. I would pray, "Lord, give me so much business that I won't even have time to sleep! I don't care if I have to work all day and all night just please bless my business." I bet you can guess what happened. The Lord gave me exactly what I asked for, I was flipping websites hand over fist. I was sleeping maybe 3 to 4 hours a night. I got so overwhelmed that I began to complain, and the Lord reminded me that this is what I prayed for. I immediately repented and never complained again. I decided I was going to do whatever it took to be successful.

You are going to get tired and you are going to get fatigued, but you have to do everything in your power to press through it. On my desk I have pictures of my two daughters and when I get tired I look at their pictures. It gives me that extra boost to keep going. It would break my heart to have to look into their eyes one day and tell them that they can't do something or have something they need because I got tired and quit working. There is no way I'm going to let that happen!

FOCUS

What is it that will keep you going when you get tired and want to quit? What or Who Is Your Why?
(Write it below)

_____

_____

_____

_____

_____

_____

_____

_____

_____

_____

_____

_____

_____

_____

_____

_____

_____

_____

_____

_____

_____

_____

_____

_____

_____

_____

_____

_____

_____

_____

_____

_____

_____

_____

_____

_____

ORGANIZATION

Get organized! Plan your next day, your next move your next step! Proper preparation prevents poor performance. Being organized is really the first step. You need to organize your thoughts, write down what you want to accomplish and why you want to accomplish it.

One day I was on the phone with TobyMac and he said to me, "Kelly the difference between us (Gotee Records) and others is, we are not machine gun shooters, we don't just throw a bunch of stuff out there and pray that we hit something. We are sharpshooters. We line up the opportunities and knock them down one by one. We wait for the right single, the right tour, and more importantly the right time to launch our artist!"

Take it from the OG himself, it pays to be organized and patient. Take your time and write out your plans and ideas. After you have them written down, organize them in the order of importance and start knocking them out one by one.

In the Space Below List 5 Things
You Want to Accomplish:

1._____

2._____

3._____

4._____

5._____

Now Write Down 5 Things You Need
To Do Every Day to Bring Those Things to Pass

1._____

2._____

3._____

4._____

5._____

Here is how I handle my daily to-do list. I don't go to bed until I have completed everything on that list. The list has to get done that day. You have to decide how bad do you want it?

OPPOSITION!

You think just because you have made up your mind to get locked-in on your dreams and goals that the universe is just going to get out of your way and make it easy for you? Haha, think again! At one point or another, all hell is going to break loose. I'm not telling you this to scare you, I'm telling you this to warn you, so you can be ready when it does happen. It's not what happens to us, it's how we deal with what happens to us that matters. If things don't go your way, are you going to quit? Are you going to whine and cry about it? I hate to have to bust your bubble, but your dreams and goals don't care about your feelings! So, pick yourself up and keep going!

"Look at life for what it is, not for what you want it to be."

If Michael Jordan didn't get cut from his high school basketball team, would he still have become Air Jordan? Would he be greatest basketball player of all time?

If Oprah Winfrey was never told she was not pretty enough to be on TV, would she still have become known as just Oprah and have a net worth of 3 billion dollars?

People are going to think you are crazy! Sometimes you are going to think you are crazy!

Stay Locked-In on Your Goal!

5 SCRIPTURES THAT WILL HELP YOU WHEN OPPOSITION COMES

Mark 9:23 - Jesus said unto him, If thou canst believe, all things are possible to him that believeth.

Jeremiah 29:11 - For I know the thoughts that I think toward you, says the Lord, thoughts of peace and not of evil, to give you a future and a hope.

Isaiah 41:10 Fear thou not; for I am with thee: be not dismayed; for I am thy God: I will strengthen thee; yea, I will help thee; yea, I will uphold thee with the right hand of my righteousness.

Isaiah 54:17 No weapon formed against you shall prosper...

Isaiah 55:11 So shall my word be that goeth forth out of my mouth: it shall not return unto me void, but it shall accomplish that which I please, and it shall prosper in the thing whereto I sent it.

HAPPY AS YOU WANT TO BE

Almost everyone has heard the hit single 'Happy' by Pharrell Williams. The song has a very catchy way of conveying its message of being happy to everyone.

Living a happy, resilient, and optimistic life is wonderful and is also good for your health. Being happy actually protects you from the stresses of life. Stress is linked to top causes of death such as heart disease, cancer, and stroke.

One of the better things ever said is - 'The only thing in life that will always remain the same is change', and in our life, we have the power to make the necessary changes if we want to. Even if we find ourselves in an unbearable situation we can always find solace in the knowledge that it too would change.

Relationships are essential to happiness. People are different, accept people for who or what they are, avoid clashes, constant arguments, and let go of all kinds of resentments. If arguments seem unavoidable, continue to make an effort to understand the situation. It's totally OK at the end of the day to protect your happiness by removing that person from your life. Happiness is actually found in everyone, increasing it is a way to make a life more wonderful and also healthier.

To be happy is relatively easy, just decide to be a happy person. Abraham Lincoln observed that most people for most of the time can choose how happy or stressed, how relaxed or troubled, how bright or dull their outlook to be. The choice is simple really, choose to be happy.

There are several ways by which you can do this.

Being grateful is a great attitude. We have so much to be thankful for. Thank God for bringing you home safely, thank the cook for a wonderful dinner and thank the guy who shared your post on social media and thank God for being alive.

Quit watching the news. The news is stressful. Some people just can't start their day without their daily dose of news. 99% of the news we hear or read is bad news. Negativity is toxic. Starting the day with bad news is not a sensible thing to do.

Manage your time wisely. Time is invaluable and too important to waste. Time management can be viewed as a list of rules that involves scheduling, setting goals, planning, creating lists of things to do, and prioritizing. These are the core basics of time management that should be understood to develop effective personal time management skills. These basic skills can be fine-tuned further to include the finer points of each skill that can give you that extra reserve to make the results you desire.

Laugh and laugh heartily every day. Have you heard a good joke? Tell your friends or family about it. As the word also says -'Laughter is the best medicine'. Spread laughter around like confetti because everyone can benefit from a good laugh. I have a friend and fellow marketer/ entrepreneur who keeps her T.V. on comedy central, whether she is watching it or not. I didn't get it at first, but she is controlling her atmosphere by filling it with laughter.

Express your feelings, affections, friendship, and passion to people around you. They will most likely reciprocate your actions. Try not to keep pent up anger or frustrations because this is bad for your health. Instead, find ways of expressing them that will not cause more injury or hurt to anyone.

Working hard brings tremendous personal satisfaction. It gives a feeling of being competent in finishing our tasks. Accomplishments are necessary for all of us, they give us a sense of value. Work on things that you feel are worthy of your time.

Learning is a joyful exercise. Try and learn something new every day. Learning also makes us expand and broaden our horizons. It could also give us more opportunities in the future.

Run, jog, walk, and do other things that your body was made for. Feel alive.

Avoid exposure to negative elements like loud noises, toxins, and hazardous places.

These are a few of the simple things you can do every day to be happy.

Lastly, always remember the quote from Abraham Lincoln, he said, "Most people are about as happy as they make up their minds to be."

CHAPTER 3

CONSISTENCY

The achievement of a level of performance that does not vary greatly in quality over time.

<u>Use Every Second of Your Day!</u>

Time equals Money! We have all heard that statement before, but I'm sure if you are a young person reading this book you don't really get it because right now to you, time is moving very slow. You can't wait to be an adult, so you can do what you want. Believe me, there is going to come a time when you realize how much time you have wasted doing nothing or hanging out with your friends, that you could have spent working on your dreams and goals.

How can you use every second of your day?

I do what I call working while I'm waiting. What that means is, while I'm waiting for my daughter to come out of the school when I'm picking her up, I have a list of things I do. I either record a motivational video, go over my to-do list for the day and see how much I have accomplished that day, I go over my calendar to see what I have coming up, or I make follow up phone calls and return emails. I think you get my point. There is always something to do, so I use every second of my day to do something productive that will get me closer to my goals.

I even work while I'm on the toilet, I either read a business book or how to book on something I need to learn that will get me closer to my living my dreams and accomplishing my goals.

In this day and age, there are really no excuses for anyone not to be successful! You can literally search Google for anything you want to know or learn about. Do you want to learn how to design websites? There are thousands of video tutorials on YouTube that will walk you through the process, step by step and show you how to do it. Do you want to learn how to use social media to grow your business or start a modeling career? Whatever it is you want to do the information is right at your fingertips. When I was coming up and we wanted to know something, the only resource we had in the house was an old set of encyclopedias that were outdated and had maybe one or two paragraphs of information on what you wanted to learn about. Technology and the Internet have changed the way we retrieve information and I love the change.

Time management is basically about being focused. The Pareto Principle, also known as the '80:20 Rule' states that 80% of efforts that are not time managed or unfocused generates only 20% of the desired output. However, 80% of the desired output can be generated using only 20% of a well time managed effort. Although the ratio '80:20' is only arbitrary, it is used to put emphasis on how much is lost or how much can be gained with time management.

Some people view time management as a list of rules that involves scheduling appointments, goal settings, thorough planning, creating things like to-do lists and prioritizing. These are the core basics of time management that should be understood to develop effective personal time management skills. These basic skills can be fine-tuned further to include the finer points of each skill, which can give you that extra reserve to produce the results you desire.

There are more skills involved in time management than the core basics. Skills like decision making, along with inherent abilities such as emotional intelligence and critical thinking are also essential to your personal growth.

Personal time management involves everything you do. No matter how big and no matter how small, everything counts. Any knowledge you acquire, each word of advice you take into a count, and each new skill you develop should be taken into consideration. It is all relative to personal growth.

Having a balanced lifestyle should be the main result of having effective personal time management. This is the vital aspect that many practitioners of personal time management fail to grasp. Time management is about getting results, not about being busy.

Effective personal time management will directly improve anyone's life in these six areas: physical, intellectual, social, career, emotional, and spiritual.

- The physical aspect involves having a healthy body, less stress, and less fatigue.

- The intellectual aspect involves learning and other mental growth activities.

- The social aspect involves developing personal or intimate relations and being an active contributor to society.

- The career aspect involves school and business.

- The emotional aspect involves appropriate feelings or desires and manifesting them.

- The spiritual aspect involves a personal quest for meaning and purpose.

Thoroughly planning and having a set of things to do and a list for each of the key areas may not be very practical, but determining which area in your life is not being given enough attention is part of time management. Each area creates the whole you. If you are ignoring one area, then you are ignoring an important part of yourself.

Personal time management should not be such a daunting task. It is a very sensible and reasonable approach to solving problems, big or small. A great way of learning time management and improving your personal life is to follow several basic activities. One of them is to review your goals, whether it be immediate or long-term goals often. A way to do this is to keep a list that is always accessible to you. Always determine which task is necessary or not necessary in achieving your goals and which activities are helping you maintain a balanced lifestyle.

Each and every one of us has a peek time and a time when we slow down, these are our natural cycles. We should be able to tell when to do the difficult tasks and when we are the sharpest.

Learning to say "No" is a major tool. You actually see this advice often. Heed to it even if it involves saying the word to family or friends. You may hurt some feelings, but in the end, it will be worth it. After all, it's up to you to protect your peace as you pursue your goals.

A Few Things to Remember...

- Pat yourself on the back or just reward yourself in any manner for an effective time management result.

- Try and get the cooperation from people around you who are actually benefiting from your efforts of time management.

- Don't procrastinate. Attend to necessary things immediately.

- Have a positive attitude and set yourself up for success. But be realistic in your approach to achieving your goals.

- Have a record or journal of all your activities. This will help you get things in their proper perspective.

- These are the initial steps you take to become a well-rounded individual.

- As they say, "Personal time management is the art and science of building a better life."

From the moment you integrate time management skills into your life, you open up several options that can provide a broad spectrum of solutions to your personal growth. It also creates more doors for opportunities to knock on.

STAY CONSISTENT BY DEVELOPING A DAILY ROUTINE

Routine - a sequence of actions regularly followed; a fixed program.

The great John Maxwell said, "You will never CHANGE YOUR LIFE until you change something you do daily. THE SECRET OF YOUR SUCCESS is found in your daily routine."

Before I ever read this quote, I developed a daily routine. This quote confirmed I was on the right path to making my dreams a reality and it also encouraged me to stick to my daily routine.

MY DAILY ROUTINE

It Can Vary Depending on The Day, but This Will Give You an Idea

6am - 7am Your normal bathroom stuff, shower, shave, brush my teeth etc.

7am - 8am Prayer, Read the Bible, Send My Family a Daily Scripter, Eat Breakfast

8am - 9am Read My Short and Long-Term Goals, Say My Affirmations Out loud, Count My Blessing

9am - 10am Post to my blog, share it on social media,

10am - 12pm Follow-ups with clients, answer emails, reach out to new clients

12pm - 1pm Lunch Meeting with Business Client or Associate

1pm - 2pm Answer emails return phone calls, Text Messages

2pm - 3pm Get in Line Pick-Up my daughters

Review Notes, Review First half of day progress

Record Motivational Video, Post an Instagram Quote

3pm - 4pm Client Projects, New Projects - work my way down the list of projects I'm working on

4pm - 5pm Edit Video, New Projects - work my way down the list of projects I'm working on

5pm - 6pm Pick up Love (My baby girl)

6pm - 7pm Edit Video

7pm - 8pm Dinner

8pm - 9pm Walk and listen to a book or Motivational audio

9pm - 10pm New Projects - work my way down the list of projects I'm working on

10pm - Write to Do list for next day

Review Daily Checklist and progress, Read My Scriptures, Goals & Affirmations

Journal - what went right, what went wrong, what can I work on, what inspired me today

Shower, Bed

"The most common trait of millionaires is they invest the first 30 to 60 minutes of the day in their body and mind. Some call it their "hour of power," others call it their "sacred 60". ~ Forbes Magazine

RID YOURSELF OF ALL DISTRACTIONS

I had a friend in high school that wanted to make it to major league to play baseball so bad that every year before baseball season he would break up with his girlfriend. Me being the immature kid I was, I told him he was stupid. Every year I knew when he did it because you would see her walking down the hallway crying her eyes out and hiding her face. I didn't get it then, but you better believe I get it now. In order to make your dreams and goals come true, you have to be selfish to some extent because you will need every ounce of your energy to focus on the task at hand. Anything that can be a distraction or drain any part of your energy, you should rid yourself of it.

Now my friend didn't make it to the major league to play baseball, but he did get a full ride to college to play and is currently a head baseball coach at a college. We can only speculate what his life would have been if he allowed his girlfriend and other peer pressure to distract him from going all in on his dream.

The faster you decide what it is you want to do and that you are going to go all out, lock-in and devote all your time, energy and will into it, the faster you will either get it or you will discover what it is that you are truly called to do.

I tried many things before I found myself and discovered what I was put on earth to do. There is nothing wrong with trying something, the problem is going after what you are trying halfcocked! GO ALL IN!

MOTIVATIONAL INTERLUDE

If you're not giving it your all in everything you do, then what are we talking about? You've got to go hard every single day. You've got to get up and lay your bricks. If you lay your bricks every day before you know it, you'll have a mansion. Slow motion is better than no motion. Keep it moving. Keep it going. Don't stop. If you're met with an obstacle, figure out how to get through the obstacle and keep going. Have no fear. Go hard. Every day you've got to lay your bricks for your foundation of your dreams. You've got to go do it. Think about your family. Think about your kids. Think about your wife. Think about your husband. Don't wait for the opportunity to knock. Leave the door open. Develop your daily routine. Get up, say your prayers, read your word, read your goals and then pursue those dreams with passion and diligence. Take steps towards your goals every single day. If you're working a 9-5, once you leave that job, you better come home and get to work on your dreams. Use your lunch break. I remember when I was working two jobs, on my lunch break at Walmart, I would go into a corner and I would work on my dreams. I would write out my plans. I would write out my goals. So, when I got home, I could put them into action. You've got to put in the work. If you don't put in the work, how do you expect for your dreams to come true? No one is going to give you nothing. You've got to work for it. If you don't work for it, you don't deserve it. Now you can do it. All you have to do is make up in your mind to make it happen. How bad do you want it? My man ET, this is one of my favorite quotes, he says, "When you want to succeed as bad as you want to breathe, then you'll be successful." You got to grind hard. You got to go get it. Every single day. Don't sleep without going after your dreams. Like I said, "Slow motion is better than no motion!" So, make a plan of action, and each day, make sure you accomplish that goal or accomplish that task and don't sleep until it's done. Go get it. Make it happen. No more excuses. If you don't know what to do, find out what to do. Find somebody that's already doing what you want to do. And emulate them. You have to be hungry, you must be relentless. You can't take no for an answer. You can't be afraid to ask for what you want. You can't be afraid to cultivate relationships. I'm telling you, this thing is about relationships, but nobody is going to do business with you if they don't see that you want it. If they don't see that you're hustling, if they don't see that you believe in your dreams, they won't be interested. I've talked to billionaires and I've interviewed millionaires. All of them want to see that the person that they're doing business is just as hungry and just as passionate as they are about doing business, about entrepreneurship, about a better life, achieving goals, and about achieving their dreams. No more excuses! Make it happen! You are not allowed to make excuses. Your job is to make it happen! Now go get it!

Who Are Your Role Models
& How Do They Inspire You?

_____

_____

_____

_____

_____

_____

_____

_____

_____

_____

_____

_____

_____

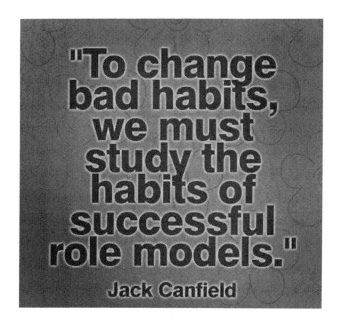

"To change bad habits, we must study the habits of successful role models."

Jack Canfield

CHAPTER 4

KEEN

Having or showing eagerness or enthusiasm.

Are you keen on what it is that you want to accomplish? Does it get you excited to get out of bed in the morning and does it keep you awake at night?

The other day I was cutting a very close friend's hair and he asked, "Did you watch the Chicago Bulls game last night?" I said, "No."

Of course, he asked, "Why not?"

I replied "Because bro, I have a goal I'm trying to meet of becoming a millionaire so I'm willing to sacrifice watching the game on TV, so I can watch it courtside when I become a millionaire. You should have seen the look on his face. I said, "I know that I sound crazy and you may think I'm over doing it, but I look at it like this Jimmy Butler and Dwayne Wade already made their millions, I'm trying to get there and every second I waste watching them on TV, I'm losing valuable time I could be using to work on my dream!"

I heard a story about (Olympic athlete gymnast) how she skipped her senior prom to prepare for the Olympics! I was like wow, she was so focused and dedicated to achieving her goal that she gave up going to her senior prom to prepare for it! I ask you again, what are you willing to give up? Some of y'all won't give up watching your favorite team play basketball or football on TV. Some of y'all won't stay out of the mall spending money you don't really have. Some of y'all won't say no now so you can say yes later! All it takes is a sacrifice now, so you can have and do what you want later. I believe it was Les Brown who said: "If you do what is hard now your life will be a lot easier and if you do what is easy now, your life is going to be a lot harder!" Some of you have done too much of the easy stuff that's why it is a little harder to focus and buckle down now. I want you to know it can be done, you just have to decide you are going to do whatever it takes to get it done. You have what it takes, but it's going to take everything you have.

My mentor and great friend Rodney Johnson said this to me and I never forgot it. He said, "In life, you can pay now, or you can pay later, but you will pay!" I added it to his quote "If you pay later there is interest!" I bet you never thought about how in life, there is interest on things you wait to take action on, like the dreams or goals you push to the side. It will be a lot harder to act the longer you wait.

Are you willing to give up friends, family members, bad habits, your normal comfortable daily routines, and traditions? No, it's not easy, but it's worth it! I remember my son who is a national Christian recording artist signed to TobyMac's Gotee Records came home from school in 7th grade and told me that he wanted to do music for the rest of his life. He said his goal was to get a record deal, travel the world singing and rapping for God. The first thing I told him was, "OK if this is truly what you want to do with your life the first thing you have to realize is you can no longer do what everybody else is doing. You can no longer entertain conversations that you know are against your beliefs. You can't go to the house parties and you can't just post anything you want on social media. Your life is a sacrifice now. He agreed and said he was going to focus on his dream. Well, he had no clue at the time what I meant, but I'm more than positive he can tell you now about how hard it was to get where he is today and how much of a daily struggle it is to stay on course. All and all, with God's grace he is doing well and I'm very proud of him.

What Are You Willing to Give Up in Order For Your Dreams to Come True?

_____

_____

_____

_____

_____

_____

_____

_____

_____

_____

_____

_____

_____

_____

_____

_____

_____

_____

_____

_____

_____

THE POWER OF SPEAKING IT

I remember attending my first NBA game, it was an exhibition between the Atlanta Hawks and New Orleans Hornets. The cool thing was the game was actually in my area at East Tennessee State University, I was so excited! Walking into the venue there was a box for a free raffle that you could enter to win a $100 gas card. I filled one out and as I was walking away I said out loud, "I'm gonna win!" So they drew a card out in between each quarter and every time they said they were getting to do the drawing I said out loud this me right here I'm about to win and before the 4th quarter they came to the middle of the court and announced they were getting ready to draw again, I stood up and said this me, I got this and sure enough, the announcer said "The winner is Kelly Cole", I raised both of my hands and said, "YES! Thank you, Lord!" I walked down the stairs and claimed my prize. That experience reminded me of the power that we all have to speak things into existence. We forget that the power and life and death is in our tongue.

You have the power to speak things into existence in your life! One of the ways I practice this every day in my life is by reciting a list of Affirmations. I say them out loud every morning. I have placed some of them on the next page, feel free to speak them over your life as well.

My Daily Affirmations

I am a Mighty Man of God
I Can Have What God Says I Can Have
I Believe Gods Word
I Speak Gods Word
I Am the Head and Not the Tail
I Am Wealthy
Money Flows to Me Naturally
I Make It Happen
I Am a Millionaire
I Am Anointed with Abundance
I Can Do All Things Through Christ!
I Am Wise and Conduct Myself in a Wise Manner
I have Peace
I Am Healed
I Am a Giver
I Am Good Ground
I Ask for What I Want
I Am a Master Salesman
I have the Favor of God on my Life
I deserve great wealth
I deserve to close $10,000 deals
I deserve to close $100,000 deals
I deserve to close $1,000,000 deals
I deserve the finer things in life
I Am Focused
I Am Determined
I AM LOCKED-IN
I have everything I need to make my dreams come true

In the Space Provide Below Write Your Own Daily Affirmations

_____

_____

_____

_____

_____

_____

_____

_____

_____

_____

_____

_____

_____

_____

_____

_____

_____

_____

_____

_____

_____

_____

_____

_____

_____

_____

_____

_____

_____

_____

_____

SPEAK FAVOR EVERYWHERE YOU GO!

Another secret to my success is I speak favor everywhere I go. Everywhere I go I believe something great is going to happen to me. I believe I will receive favor in some way.

This past June I decided to surprise my daughter with tickets to Jermaine Dupree's *The Rap Game – So So Summer 17 Tour*. When I purchased the tickets, they were sold out of the gold VIP tickets, so I purchased the silver package. The biggest difference was with the gold VIP you got to take individual pictures with the performers, which I didn't think was a big deal until we got there, and they told all of us we could possibly end up in a picture with strangers. So, they separated the gold from the silver and put us in two lines. While standing in-line, I said in my spirit, "Favor Lord." I promise the next thing I know, a lady who we were standing in line with before they opened the doors, walked up to me and my daughter and handed us 2 gold VIP wristbands and said her two friends she purchased them for didn't show up. I smiled and said, "Thank you so much!" Of course, my baby girl was ecstatic! Then I looked up and said, "Thank you, Lord." because I knew it was Him who had given me this favor.

Another one of my favorite examples of speaking things into existence is when my sister Keke went to a Kanye West concert. At the time, she was a broke undergraduate college student. The concert was announced and from that moment, she kept saying, "I'm going to that concert and I don't know how. And I will be in the front row!" She chatted with classmates about the upcoming concert and no one was as excited as she was to get to this concert.

Days go by and the concert is sold out. She still doesn't have any money or the tickets. Even still, she kept saying, "I'm going to that concert and I don't know how. And I will be in the front row!"

A few days before the concert, her best friend says, "I want to give you your present early because I won't be around for your actual birthday." Later on, they met up and I bet you guessed it…the birthday gift was two tickets to see Kanye West. My sister was elated, to say the least. Now, these tickets were general admission, so the chances of being front and center were slim to none. That didn't stop my sister from saying, "I'm going to that concert and I will be in the front row!"

The day of the concert, she accidentally left her identification at school. By the time she realized it, the campus had already closed for the day and there was no way she could get into the Student Government Office to retrieve it from her desk. After much deliberation, she asked our first cousin to borrow her ID and she agreed. The funny thing is, my sister was easily 100 pounds heavier than our cousin, but it worked. The security at the concert didn't hesitate to let her in. She was running late, so there was no way she would get a front row spot to see Kanye with all of the people ahead of her. She waited patiently to get into the building and although at least 150 people entered before her, they didn't seem to be interested in getting to the front row. They happened to fill the outer portion of the room, which meant she could walk right up to the railing directly in front of the stage to enjoy the concert.

She enjoyed the concert with a friend that happened to be just as Kanye crazy as she was. They both went to concert broke and enjoyed themselves as if they didn't have a care in the world. They happened to discuss their plans to get home because my sister's friend was concerned about going home so late on public transportation. My sister assured her friend, "Girl, we are going to get home, just fine because I'm going to see someone I know, and they will give us a ride." This was just my sister talking, she wasn't already aware that anyone she knew was there, she just said it. Low and behold, she happens to turn around at a certain point and sees an old friend that lives on the same block as her friend. They chatted, and the old friend offered them a ride and the rest is history.

If all of us would get this worked up over our goals and dreams to have the audacity to speak what we want to happen and walk toward it, things will fall into place. Dr. Martin Luther King Jr. said it best, "Faith is taking the first step, even when you don't see the whole staircase." My sister had her outfit prepared without even having a ticket. She was broke, left her ID and ended up getting to the concert late, but she got there, experienced the concert up close and personal, and got a safe ride home. With that being said, I want you to make room for the Grammy Award. Go open the business bank account. Buy you those pants that are a few sizes smaller and make room for even more clothes. Whatever the goal, take a step in that direction as you speak the results you desire!

DON'T TAKE SHORTCUTS

If you are not going to give it your all, don't do it at all!

My dad used to say, "When you take a shortcut, you will end up cut short!" I never forgot that. Taking shortcuts leads to only temporary success and temporary reward. It doesn't last. It gives the false feeling of celebration, but you know deep inside that you didn't earn it. When you make up in your mind what it is you want, you need to decide at that very moment that you are going to do what it is that you will have to do to make it happen.

The reason you may want to take a shortcut is that you feel like you are behind. Let me reassure you, YOU ARE NOT LATE! As long as you are taking consistent action every day, you will get there. Be patient, but engage in consistent action. Your speed does not matter, Forward is FORWARD!

Stop looking to the left or right, get off social media looking at what everyone else is doing, focus on you. It's easy to lose focus by looking at someone else's harvest. The Lord said, "Lift up your head your harvest is ripe already." You can't see what he has already given you because you are looking at someone else's harvest. Focus on your lane and do what he has called you to do. There are a group of people who you are called to, serve them and that place is where you will find your harvest!

CHAPTER 5

EVOLVE

Evolve, grow daily, and strive to be a more effective leader.

In the daily hustle and bustle, do you feel that your goals remain just that – goals? Then maybe it's time for you to stand up and do something about it. Most people are content just to stand around listening to orders and it isn't unusual to adopt a follow-the-leader mentality. But maybe, somewhere inside of you, you feel the desire to make things happen – to be the head, not the tail. If that's the case, then maybe leadership suits you just fine.

Some people believe that great leaders are made, not born. Yes, it may be true that some people are born with natural talents. However, without practice, without drive, without enthusiasm, and without experience, there can be no true development in leadership. You must also remember that good leaders are continually working and studying to improve their natural skills. This takes a commitment to constantly improve in whatever endeavor a person chooses.

First of all, let's define leadership. To be a leader, one must be able to influence others to accomplish a goal or an objective. He or she contributes to the organization and cohesion of a group. Contrary to what most people believe, leadership is not about power. It is not about harassing people or driving them using fear. It is about encouraging others towards the goal. It is putting everyone on the same page and helping them see the big picture. You must be a leader, not a boss.

First of all, you have to get people to follow you. How is this accomplished? People follow others when they see a clear sense of purpose. People will only follow you if they see that you know where you are going. Remember that bumper sticker? The one that says, don't follow me, I'm lost too! The same holds true for leadership. If you do not know where you're headed to, chances are people will not follow you at all.

You must have a clear vision of where you are going. Having a clear sense of hierarchy, knowing who the bosses are, who to talk to, the goals and objectives, and how everything works are the only ways to show others that you know what you are doing. Being a leader is not about what you make others do. It's about who you are, what you know, and what you do. You are a reflection of what your subordinates must be.

Studies have shown that another basis of good leadership is the trust and confidence your subordinates have in you. If they trust you, they will go through hell and high water for you and for the common goal. Trust and confidence are built on good relationships, trustworthiness, and high ethics. The way you deal with your people, and the relationships you build will lay the foundation for the strength of your group. The stronger your relationship, the stronger their trust and confidence are in your capabilities. Once you have their trust and confidence, you may now proceed to communicate the goals and objectives you are to undertake.

Communication is a very important key to good leadership. Without this, you cannot be a good leader. The knowledge and technical expertise you have must be clearly imparted to other people. When there are deadlines to meet, projects to complete, and tasks to master, your team will need clear

Be aware of the fact that you cannot be a good leader and unless you have good judgment. You must be able to assess situations, weigh the pros and cons of any decision, and actively seek out a solution. It is this judgment that your subordinates will come to rely upon. Therefore, good decision-making is vital to your success.

Leaders are not do-it-all heroes. You should not claim to know everything, and you should not rely on your skills alone. It is not about just you. It is about you and the people around you. You should recognize and take advantage of the skills and talents your subordinates have. Once you come to this realization will you be able to work as one cohesive unit.

Being a great leader takes a good deal of work and time. It is not learned overnight. Do you have the drive and the desire to serve required of leaders? Do you have the desire to work cooperatively with other people? Then start now. Take your stand and be a leader today.

Take Good Care of Yourself

It's much easier to be positive when you are eating well, exercising, and getting enough rest. I have to be honest with you, this is one of my biggest struggles. I love to eat! I especially love Chinese food, Soul food, and Mexican food! HAHA! I like it all except seafood. My daily struggle is to choose the healthy options that are available and to walk at least 1hr a day. There is no excuse for it because I actually feel good when I do the things I know I should be doing. Deon Sanders said it like this, "When you look good you feel good, when you feel good you sell good!" That is so true! When my clothes are fitting just right, and I feel good on the inside I have the best days. When I haven't been eating right nor exercising, I tend to not do as well.

Eating healthy or exercising may not be tough for you, but if they are the same principles apply: You need to write down a clear goal, you need to read that goal every day and you need to take the necessary action daily to make your weight loss goal happen.

HEALTH IS WEALTH

CHAPTER 6

DETERMINED

Don't Take No for An Answer

When it comes to getting something you want, don't take no for answer! Figure out how to get what you want. Be persistent in your pursuit of your goals and dreams.

One of my favor scriptures in the Amplified version says it like this "Ask and keep on asking and it will be given to you; seek and keep on seeking and you will find; knock and keep on knocking and the door will be opened to you. 8 For everyone who keeps on asking receives, and he who keeps on seeking finds, and to him who keeps on knocking, it will be opened." Matthew 7:7-8 (AMP)

You have to ask and keep on asking, seek and keep on seeking, knock and keep on knocking! Most people I encounter ask one time and if they get a no they don't ask again. They look in one place and if what they are looking for does jump out and come to them, they stop seeking. If they knock one time and nobody answers the door, they leave. I can promise you this: with that type of attitude and work ethic you will never be successful.

One of my favorite movies is the movie *Rudy*. If you have never seen it, I command you to go watch it after you finish reading this book. What I love about the movie is everything about Rudy didn't add up for him to reach his goal to be a Notre Dame football player, but that didn't stop him from going after his dream. His dad, his brother, his teachers, and high school coaches all told him he was crazy and that it would never happen, but he didn't let that stop him from giving it his all!

Side note: In your pursuit of your dreams control what you can control and let the things you can't control work themselves out. You can show up on time, you can outwork everyone, you can give everything you have, you can have the right attitude and just watch what happens when you do so.

Rudy left home and went to South Bend, Indiana with little to no money. He didn't know anybody, and he hadn't even registered for the school. He didn't have the grades to even get in the school, but none of that stopped him from going after his dream. But here you are with all of these tools and resources available and, yet you won't take the first step in going after your dream. You won't simply ask, seek the answers and knock on a few doors. Let's be completely frank. You have Google! You can literally go to your local library if you don't have the internet or a computer and get on theirs and search google for whatever it is you want to learn about or become. Let's take it a step further, Google owns YouTube, there are thousands of free video tutorials on YouTube that will teach you how to do almost anything you can imagine. So, do you really have an excuse for why you can't be successful?

Be Diligent

You can't be slack in something's and diligent in others

"The way you do one thing is the way you do EVERYTHING."

I'm not going to tell you the rest of the movie *Rudy* because I want you to watch it and cry like do every time I watch it. I do want to share the back story of *Rudy* and how diligent he was in all areas of life, not just when it came to playing football.

It took Rudy nine years to get the movie made. Friends laughed at him and told him it would never happen. He was cutting grass one day and they drove by mocking him and said, "Hey Hollywood star when is your movie coming out?" He got fed up, sold everything he had and bought a ticket to California. He knocked on doors for over three years, slept on benches, and got kicked out of places over 500 times. After a while, he started sleeping on a couch in the bottom of the hotel until a bellboy made him leave. The bellboy asked him what he was doing. He said "I'm trying to get a movie done about my life. The bellboy gave him his brother-in-laws' number, who just happened to be the same guy who produced the movie *Hoosiers*, Angelo Pizzo. What a coincidence. Rudy called him every day for a year but Mr. Pizzo never called him back!

Finally, one-day Mr. Pizzo answers the phone and makes Rudy a deal. The deal was that if he agrees to meet him for dinner, Rudy would stop calling. Of course, Rudy agreed and said, "Yes." Mr. Pizzo said, "Ok I'll meet u for dinner but I'm not going to make your movie, I just want u to stop calling me." Rudy agreed to meet at 7 p.m. Rudy stayed at the restaurant until almost midnight and the guy never showed up. As he was leaving, he got stopped by a mailman. The mailman asks him "What's going on?" Rudy didn't really feel like talking, but he told him he was supposed to meet Mr. Pizzo for dinner and he assumes he forgot it. The mailman said, "I know Mr. Pizzo, I've been delivering his mail for years! He lives right there across the street!"

Rudy runs and knocks on the door. Mr. Pizzo was in such shock and asked Rudy, "How do you keep finding me?" Rudy goes into his spill, Mr. Pizzo invites Rudy in and ends up doing Rudy's film! Rudy made up in his mind that he would not be denied! It took him nine years of struggle, pain, and commitment to make it happen, but he Got-Locked In and made it happen.

What could you accomplish if you made up in your mind you won't be denied?

_____

_____

_____

_____

_____

_____

_____

_____

_____

_____

CHAPTER 7

INVESTIGATE

Find Solutions

How many times have you caught yourself saying "There could be no other solution to a problem and that the problem leads to a dead end?" How many times have you felt stumped knowing that the problem before you is one you cannot solve. No leads. No options. No solutions.

Did it feel like you had exhausted all possible options and, yet you are still standing in front of the mountain – large, unconquerable, and impregnable? When encountering such an enormous problem, you may feel like you're hammering against a steel mountain. The pressure of having to solve such a problem may be overwhelming.

Rejoice! There is yet hope! With some creative problem-solving techniques, you may be able to look at your problem in a different light and that light might just be the end of the tunnel that leads to possible solutions. I'm aware that it sounds cliché, but it's true.

First of all, in the light of creative problem-solving, you must be open-minded to the fact that there may be more than just one solution to the problem. In addition, you must be open to the fact that there may be solutions to problems you thought were unsolvable. Now, with this optimistic mindset, we can try to be a little bit more creative in solving our problems.

1. Maybe the reason we cannot solve our problems is that we have not really taken a hard look at what the problem is. Here, trying to understand the problem and having a concrete understanding of its workings is integral to solving the problem. If you know how it works, then you have a better foundation towards solving the problem. Not trying to make the simple statement of what problem is. Try to identify the participating entities and what their relationships with one another are. Take note of the things you stand to gain any stand to lose from the current problem. Now you have a simple statement of what the problem is.

2. Try to take note of all the constraints and assumptions you have concerning the problem. Sometimes it is these assumptions that obstruct our view of possible solutions. You have to identify which assumptions are valid and which assumptions need to be addressed.

3. Try to solve the problem in parts. Solve it going from the general view towards the more detailed parts of the problem. This is called the top-down approach. Write down the question and then come up with a one-sentence solution. The solution should be a general statement of what will solve the problem. From this point, you can develop the solution further and increase the complexity little by little.

4. Although it helps to have critical thinking aboard as you solve a problem, you must also keep a creative, analytical voice at the back of your head. When

someone comes up with a prospective solution, try to think of how you could make that solution work. Try to be creative. At the same time, look for kinks in the armor of that solution.

5. It pays to remember that there may be more than just one solution being developed at a given time. Try to keep track of all the solutions and their developments. Remember, there may be more than just one solution to the problem.

6. Remember that old adage,"two heads are better than one." That statement is truer than it sounds. Always be open to new ideas. You can only benefit from listening to all the ideas each person has to offer. This is especially true when the person you're talking to has had experience solving problems similar to the one you are dealing with.

You don't have to be a gung-ho, solo hero to solve the problem. If you can organize collective thought on the subject, it would be much better.

7. Be patient. As long as you persevere, there is always a chance that a solution will present itself. Remember that no one was able to create an invention the first time around.

Creative thinking exercises can also help you in your quest to be a more creative problems solver.

Here is one example:

Take a piece of paper and write any word that comes to mind at the center. Now, look at that word then write the first two words that come to your mind. This can go on until you can build a tree of related words. This helps you build analytical skills and fortify your creative processes.

So, next time you see a problem you think you can not solved, think again. The solution might just be staring you right in the face. All it takes is just a little creative thinking, some planning, and a whole lot of work.

BE INNOVATIVE

I t's a talent that everyone has, yet they think they don't. It's the power of innovation. If you've ever marveled at somebody's creative prowess, guess what? You can create and innovate too. It just takes time. Everyone is born creative. The box of crayons in kindergarten was not limited to those who possessed specific potential because the truth is, everybody has potential.

You know how long it took to learn to ride a bike or drive or to never commit the same mistake again? It's the same with innovation. It takes a bit of practice and a lot of time before this mental function works easily when called upon.

Don't listen to what other people say. Follow the beat of your own drum. Allowing for the input of other people will only bring cacophony to the music you are trying to make. If you have an original idea, don't waste your time and effort trying to make people understand. They won't. And the help you will probably get comes in the form of negative feedback. If all those geniuses listened to their peers, we would probably still be living in the middle ages.

Spend time on it. I cannot stress that enough! Please do not mistake this tip as a sign telling you to quit your day job entirely. Do not! This involves some tricky time management, but with a little discipline, you'll be able to squeeze both in.

Exercise. Take a walk. Run a mile or two. Send all those endorphins coursing through your veins. Exercising certainly clears your mind, allows you to relax, and room for anything to pop up.

Record your dreams. Aren't some of your dreams just the craziest scenarios that your conscious mind would never have thought of? If you've had these dreams before, and I'm sure have, this only shows you the untapped innovative power you have lying within. So, jot down those notes. Those dreams may just create an innovative spark within you.

Find your own style. You can always tell a Van Gogh from a Matisse. You'll know Hemingway wrote something by the choice of words on the paper and it is the same with you. People will appreciate your innovation more because it is uniquely yours and that no one else would have thought of what you were thinking. That will also let people see how valuable an asset you are.

Don't hide behind nifty gadgets or tools. You don't need the most expensive set of paints to produce a masterpiece. The same way with writing. You don't need some expensive fountain pen and really smooth paper for a bestseller. In fact, J.K. Rowling wrote the first book of the *Harry Potter* Series on bits of tissue. So, what if you've got an expensive SLR camera and you're a crappy photographer? Who cares if you've got a blinged out laptop if you can't write at all? The artist actually reduces the number of tools he has as he gets better at his craft because he knows what works and what doesn't.

Nothing will work without passion. What wakes you up in the mornings? What keeps the flame burning? What is the one thing that you'll die if you don't do? Sometimes people with talent are overtaken by the people who want it more. Think about the hare and the tortoise. Sometimes you just want something so bad you become virtually unstoppable. That is undeniable passion. Passion will keep you going.

Don't worry about inspiration. You can't force it! Inspiration hits when you least expect it to and you should prepare for those unpredictable yet, inevitable moments. An idea could strike you on the way home in the car, yet alas, you poor unfortunate soul; you have no sheet of paper to scribble down a thought that could change the world. Avoid these disasters. Have a pen and paper within your arm's reach at all times. Always keep enough room in your phone to jot your ideas in it as well.

Keep in mind that you're doing these things for your own satisfaction and not anybody else's. Soon enough, they will notice, and everything should snowball from there.

What Is the Legacy You Plan on Leaving Behind?

_____

_____

_____

_____

_____

_____

_____

_____

_____

_____

_____

How Do You Want People to Remember You, Especially Your Loved Ones?

_____

_____

_____

_____

_____

_____

_____

_____

_____

_____

_____

_____

_____

_____

CHAPTER 8

NO

Get comfortable saying no to people without feeling guilty or explaining yourself.

S ay "No!" to going out to eat! Say "No!" to playing video games! Say "No!" to partying! Say "No!" to just chilling! You don't have time to chill! You have a goal and a dream! Seconds cannot be wasted! Say "No!" for now so you can live the rest of your life like the King or Queen that you are. Say "No!" to anyone that is trying to get you to do something outside of the boundaries you have set for yourself!

Stay on your grind no matter what!

Here is a lesson I learned the hard way, stay locked-in on your goal no matter who or what tells anything different. At one point early in our marriage, my wife and I were so locked in on achieving our financial goal that nothing was going to stop us! We were living below our means. We only bought the things we needed. We were not eating out and shopping. We went to work, had a side hustle, and kept putting money in the bank. At the time, I was working at Wal-Mart, plus cutting hair on the weekends. My wife was working as well. I was making so much money cutting hair and selling stuff at my shop that we were living off that money and putting our work checks in the bank. We were stacking!

I remember we were in a church service on a Wednesday night, not too long after I had given my life to Christ. I was a babe in the Lord and I didn't know much of anything. So, they have an alter call and my wife and I go up for prayer. The prophet tells us, "It's time to eat, drink, and enjoy the fruits of your labor." Now, what do you think that meant to a 22yr old and 20yr old babe in Christ? You got it! SPEND! We went from having close to $10,000 liquid in the bank to being $30,000 in debt and filing for bankruptcy. We were eating out, taking trips, shopping, and buying things we didn't need. That's what you call "Balling out of control"! After we filed for bankruptcy I vowed never again! Now the truth is that was a word out of season, it was not the time for us to eat, drink, and enjoy the fruits of labor. Why? Because we had not reached our goal! We should have taken that word as confirmation that we were on the right track and soon it would be time to eat, drink, and enjoy the fruits of our labor.

I've learned over the years it's OK to say no and not feel guilty about being selfish with your time, energy, and space. People are going to talk about you anyway, so why not live your life for you doing or not doing whatever it is that you want. You have the right to say "No!" You have the right to change your mind. My therapist had to flat-out tell me this year "Stop doing things you don't want to!" When she said it, something clicked for me and I said to myself, "You know what, she's right!"

Get Locked-In on Your Finances

I was talking to a friend the other day who was about to have his second child. He was concerned that he didn't have enough money saved, nor was he comfortable about the amount of income that was coming into the household. So, I began to share some of the wisdom I've learned from doing it all wrong for so many years. I shared what I wished someone would have shared with me.

The first thing I shared with him was the earlier you start managing your money well, the better off you will be. It really doesn't matter where you are in life because you can get on track with discipline, sacrifice, and focus. I asked him, "What if you didn't spend any money on another but what you had to, for the next year? Meaning, you paid your monthly bills and that's it. What if you didn't go to the movies, didn't go out to eat unless someone else is paying, didn't buy new clothes, or not go to concerts? Try spending nothing but what you absolutely must spend. If you did that for one year just to get out of debt, build your savings and create a cash flow, how would the rest of life be knowing that if you do decide to go out to dinner, you don't have to worry about if you will have enough money for the light bill? All it takes is a short sacrifice to get things on track, after that it's just maintaining the cash flow. The key is to be able to do and buy what you want, but not go broke in the process."

Where I come from to live paycheck to paycheck was and is a way of life. There is no planning for the future in the hood. The general mentality is: "If them new J's come out on Friday I'm getting them! I'll deal with paying the rent or the light bill later." This is not fictional, this happens every week in the hood. Their net worth is either on their feet or on their back. It's time for a change. Here is the answer, STOP spending money that you don't have! That simple. Save your money, keep your eyes open for an opportunity to invest in something that will ideally make you passive income, like a piece of real estate. Think about it every year there will be a new Mercedes. In 2019, 2020, and 2021, there will be new Air Jordan sneakers, new coach bags, Fendi bags whatever it is that you like. Every year there will be a new one. Think about this, God is not making any more land! You need to take the money you are wasting and buy some real estate to either rent out for monthly passive income or you can buy property renovate them and sell them. If you are saying to yourself, "I don't know how to do that.", use Google and YouTube to figure it out! There are no excuses!

The Money Goal

"Anytime that you talk to Kelly Cole, he always sparks something. I'm going to start calling Kelly Cole the generator. That's what I'm going to start calling him. He's going to be known as the generator. Because every time you talk to him, God uses him to generate something. I don't care if it's new ideas, new concepts. If it's new brands, new something. This guy is called the generator."
– Mo Stegall

Here is the money goal and I call this simple mathematics. I think a lot of people forget to look at things in a simple way like this. Now you never want to leave home without your product (whatever it is you sell) because you have a daily goal to make you some money. Starting out let's focus on making only an extra $100 a day, that's $3,000 a month. Now, I don't care who you are. An extra

$3000 a month will change your life tremendously. That's a mortgage payment on a 5-bedroom house (depending on the area) and if you wanted to drive a Lexus and a Benz, that's a Lexus and a Benz payment, just making $100 per day.

Now, let's break it down even simpler. Find something that you can sell for only $10. 10 of X at $10 a pop = 3,000 a month. Tell me you can't do that with as many people you encounter every day, plus just multiply it if you're promoting yourself online every day. So, 10 of X at $10 equals $100 a day and $3,000 a month. Let's say you're selling T-shirts. That's 5 T-shirts at $20 each. It equals $100 a day and $3,000 a month. What if you just duplicated your effort, hustled hard and you focus on making $200 a day? That's $6,000 a month. Focusing on making $200 a day from all of the different income streams and merchandise you create. Now, that's just 20 of X at $10 a piece or 10 T-shirts at $20 apiece. These simple equations can be applied to any form of entrepreneurship. This can be done with any product or service. I don't care if you are cleaning carpet, have a goal to make a minimum of $200 a day and at the end of the month, you will have $6,000, in a year you will have $72,000.

Now, let's look at it this way. Some days you might go the whole day and only make $50, but guess what, there's going to be a day that you make an extra $150 that will make up for that $150 that you didn't make that day. The important thing is you have to have a daily goal to at least make that $100 and when you really start picking up things and you're on your grind, you want to make that $200 day. That's $6,000 a month. Simple mathematics ladies and gentlemen.

Easy Way to Save Money

52-Week Money Challenge

WEEK	DEPOSIT AMOUNT	ACCOUNT BALANCE	WEEK	DEPOSIT AMOUNT	ACCOUNT BALANCE
1	$1.00	$1.00	27	$27.00	$378.00
2	$2.00	$3.00	28	$28.00	$406.00
3	$3.00	$6.00	29	$29.00	$435.00
4	$4.00	$10.00	30	$30.00	$465.00
5	$5.00	$15.00	31	$31.00	$496.00
6	$6.00	$21.00	32	$32.00	$528.00
7	$7.00	$28.00	33	$33.00	$561.00
8	$8.00	$36.00	34	$34.00	$595.00
9	$9.00	$45.00	35	$35.00	$630.00
10	$10.00	$55.00	36	$36.00	$666.00
11	$11.00	$66.00	37	$37.00	$703.00
12	$12.00	$78.00	38	$38.00	$741.00
13	$13.00	$91.00	39	$39.00	$780.00
14	$14.00	$105.00	40	$40.00	$820.00
15	$15.00	$120.00	41	$41.00	$861.00
16	$16.00	$136.00	42	$42.00	$903.00
17	$17.00	$153.00	43	$43.00	$946.00
18	$18.00	$171.00	44	$44.00	$990.00
19	$19.00	$190.00	45	$45.00	$1035.00
20	$20.00	$210.00	46	$46.00	$1081.00
21	$21.00	$231.00	47	$47.00	$1128.00
22	$22.00	$253.00	48	$48.00	$1176.00
23	$23.00	$276.00	49	$49.00	$1225.00
24	$24.00	$300.00	50	$50.00	$1275.00
25	$25.00	$325.00	51	$51.00	$1326.00
26	$26.00	$351.00	52	$52.00	$1378.00

Each week save the amount listed next to each week of the year and at the end of the year, you will have saved $1,378.00!

GET

LOOK
OUTWORK
CONSISTENCY
KEEN
EVOLVE
DETERMINED

INVESTIGATE
NO

It's in You

What it takes to be successful is already in you!

Russell Herman Conwell was born in 1843. He became a lawyer, then a newspaper editor, and finally a clergyman. During his lifetime, he had a profound effect on millions of people.

One day, a group of boys came to Dr. Conwell at his church and asked him if he would be willing to instruct them in college courses. They wanted a college education but lacked the money to pay for it. He told them that he'd do all he could. As the boys left, an idea began to form in Dr. Conwell's mind. He asked himself, "Why couldn't there be a fine college for poor, yet deserving young men. It was a great idea and he went to work on it at once.

Almost single-handedly, Dr. Conwell raised $7 million with which he founded one of the world's leading universities. He raised the money by giving more than 6,000 lectures all over the country. At each lecture, he told the story called "Acres of Diamonds." The story was the account of an African farmer who heard tales about other settlers who had made millions by discovering diamond mines. These tales were so exciting to the farmer that he could hardly wait to sell his farm and search for diamonds himself.

So, he sold his farm and spent the rest of his life wandering the vast African continent searching unsuccessfully for the gleaming gems which brought such high prices on the market to the world. Finally, in a fit of despondency, broke, and desperate as I remember the story, he threw himself into a river and drowned.

Meanwhile, the man who had bought his farm found a large and unusual stone in the stream which cut through the property. The stone turned out to be a great valuable diamond. Then he discovered that the farm was covered with them. Later it was to become one of the world's richest diamond mines.

The first farmer had literally owned acres of diamonds but had sold them for practically nothing in order to look for them elsewhere. If he'd only taken the time to study and prepare himself to learn what diamonds looked like in their rough state and if he had thoroughly explored the land he owned, he would have found the millions he sought right on his own property.

The thing about this story that so profoundly affected Dr. Conwell and subsequently millions of others was the idea that each of us is at this moment standing in the middle of his own acres of diamonds. If we would only have the wisdom and patience to intelligently and effectively explore the work in which we're now engaged, we'll usually find that it contains the riches we seek, whether they be financial or intangible or both.

There's nothing more pitiful in mind than the person who wastes his life running from one thing to another forever looking for the pot of gold at the end of the rainbow and never stay with one thing long enough to find it. No matter what your goal may be, perhaps the road to it can be found in the very thing in which you're currently engaged in.

You see, the average man believes some businesses are better than others instead of realizing the truth that there are no bad businesses. There are just those people who don't know enough to see the opportunities in the work they're in. No matter what your work happens to be, it's your business. You are the manager. If there seems to be no future or opportunity in it, it isn't always because it's not there, but perhaps only because you can't see it.

A farmer once poked a tiny pumpkin into an empty jug. The pumpkin grew until it completely filled the jug and couldn't grow anymore. When the farmer broke the glass, he had a pumpkin exactly the size and shape of the jug. If we're not careful, each of us can do a similar thing. We can mistakenly poke ourselves into jugs that limit our growth and shape us into these oddly shaped beings that only operate at minimal capacity. But it is us that does the poking. It's not the job, not the company, nor the territory, nor the economy, nor the times. We do it.

People who become outstanding at their work are those who see their work as an opportunity for growth and development and who prepare themselves for the opportunities which surround them every day. Preparation is the key. This means becoming so good, so competent at what we're doing now, we will actually force the opportunities we seek to come our way. It takes imagination, creative imagination, to know that diamonds don't look like diamonds in their rough state. Nor does a pile of iron ore look like iron or steel. Great opportunities lurk constantly in every aspect of the work in which we find ourselves now.

In order to begin prospecting your acres of diamonds, start to develop a faculty called "Intelligent Objectivity." The ability to stand off and look at what you do as a stranger might. Perhaps, a stranger who considers your pasture greener than his own. To do this, start at the beginning. What industry or profession does what you do fall? Do you know all you can know about your industry? How did it begin? Why did it begin? Who started it and when? What's your industry's annual revenue? How fast has it grown during the past 20 years? What's the projected growth during the next 10 years?

In short, start now to become a student of your industry. You'll be amazed at the results. In five years or less, you can become a national expert in your field. And it's the experts who write their own tickets in life. Surveys indicate that the great majority of people seem to look at what they are currently doing as the furthest they can go or as the end of the line. They need to realize how desperately an expanding and dynamic industry needs and seeks the uncommon person who is prepared to share in its growth. How richly will this person of vision and action will be rewarded? Immeasurably!

On the other hand, those who are not preparing and growing are not just standing still, in relation to their industry, they're going backward. So, ask yourself, "Do I know as much about my job and my industry as a good doctor or lawyer knows about his job or his profession?" You should, you know. This is the attitude of the person who wants to become a professional at what he does for a living. It's far more fun, many times more rewarding and interesting when you have that attitude. The real pro can ride out occasional storms in the economic seas in a safe boat built of research and preparation.

In order to become a professional in a world of amateurs, we need to study three important subjects. One thing is our company and the industry in which it operates. The second is what we do and perhaps the next step upward in our career. Lastly, we need to study people, since successfully serving and getting along with people will determine our success or failure.

Frequently, all you need to make an enormous improvement is simply a reminder of things you've known but have forgotten. Perhaps a study and research in your niche, your industry, and ways of increasing your service to others sounds like a big job. Well, it is, but it's fascinating, and in the long run, it pays tremendous dividends, builds complete security, and it can be accomplished in an hour a day devoted to reading and making permanent notes.

Think of ways and means in which you can increase your contribution to your company, your industry, and those whom you serve. You'll begin to notice a wonderful change in your world, for as you sow, so shall you reap. This applies just as much to the family as it does to the breadwinner.

The minute you adopt this attitude, you've joined the top 5% of the people of the world. You've virtually removed all competition. You're creating, rather than competing. You're affecting life, rather than just being affected by it. You're becoming a creator and a giver to life, instead of just a receiver.

By taking this attitude toward your work, your company, and industry, you're automatically taking care of two vital parts of successful living. First, you'll find yourself becoming more interested and enthusiastic about your work and its future. Beware: both interest and enthusiasm are contagious. Second of all, you're building financial security which will last a lifetime.

So, keep this thought in mind as often as you can on and off the job: Somewhere in your present work, there lurks an opportunity which will bring you everything you could possibly want for yourself and your family. It will not be labeled opportunity. It will be hidden in common everyday garments, just as well as the hairpin with which a man fashioned the first paperclip or the dirty drinking glass which triggered the paper cup industry.

Now in closing, here are 12 points to remember:

1) If we develop the wisdom and patience to intelligently and effectively explore the work in which we're now engaged, we will very likely find it contains the riches, tangible or intangible, we seek.

2) Before we go running off into what we think is a greener pasture, let's realize our own pasture is probably unlimited.

3) There are no bad businesses. It's the way in which we go about our work that makes it good or bad.

4) Let's not poke ourselves into jugs beyond which we cannot grow. Let's avoid self-limitation.

5) Only preparation can ensure we are taking advantage of

the opportunities which will present themselves in the future. Opportunities which are around us now. Let's begin to prepare now.

6) Put your imagination to work on the many ways and means of improving what you're now doing.

7) Learn all you can about what you do, your company, and your niche.

8) Since there's no limit to the growth of your industry, there's similarly no limit to your growth potential within that industry.

9) Our dynamic and growing economy needs and will well reward the uncommon person who prepares for a place in its growth.

10) Begin to build your library of reference material pertaining to what you do, your industry, your niche, and on how to better serve and get along with people.

11) Set aside an hour a day for the study and research.

12) Remember the story of the Acres of Diamonds.

Practical Tips for Writing A Book In 2 Weeks or Less!

Every year the # 1 New Year's resolution in the world is for people to write a book.

What I have noticed from being a book publisher for over 10yrs is that the most pressing problem most people have that want to write a book is actually writing the book. Their biggest excuse is they don't have the time or know where to start. So, I created this solution to solve both problems. I have created a step by step plan anyone can follow to write their book and get it published in 2 weeks or less. I have also shared some of my generator bonus tips that can even cut the time even shorter.

Part 1 – How to Get Started on Writing Your Book

Below Is a Step by Step Checklist on What to Do

- **Choose Topic / Title** (Choosing what you will write about is more important in the beginning than choosing the title. The title could change by the end of the book.)

- **Write an Outline** – The outline should include chapter titles. (Think about what you want to cover in your book. Are there things you know you want to include? Write them down as chapter titles.)

- **Research Your Topic** – Make note of sources. If you have an audience or a following, you can survey your audience, ask them what questions they have about your topic and create chapter titles around their questions if you haven't already addressed them in one of your chapters.

- **Start Writing** – Spend at least thirty minutes to an hour a day filling in the chapters. Set a goal to write at least 500 words per day.

- **Proofread** – After you finish filling in the chapters proofread it to see if you would like to add anything to what you wrote in the chapters.

- **Copyright Book** – Go to copyright.gov and pay $35 to do an electronic copyright filing on your book. If you don't have the money right now, mail yourself a sealed copy of your printed manuscript. Do not open the envelope when you receive it. It will act as a temporary copyright.

- **Send Your Book to An Editor** – After you have filed for your copyright, then you can send it to a professional book editor and have them edit your book.

- **Review the Editor's Work** – After you receive your book back from the editor, it is very important that you review what they have done. Make sure that the book was edited in the way you instructed them.

- **Format Your Book** – After your book edit is complete and your manuscript is ready, now it is time to get your book formatted for the correct book size. Some of the most popular sizes are 6x9, 5.5x8.5 & 5x8. Be sure and check with the editor of your book, most of the time a good editor will also format it for you as well.

- **Design Your Book Cover** – The next step is getting your book cover designed by a professional graphic designer. Be sure and write a clear description of what you want your cover to look like and let the design be creative in bringing it to life.

- **Choose A Publisher** – After you have all the pieces it is time to decide how you are going to publish it. Are you going to self-publish? If so, which self-publisher are you going to go with?

- **Submit Your Manuscript** – After you decide on the publisher you are going to go with, you then will need to send them your manuscript.

- **Set Book Launch date** – After you submit your manuscript and the publisher has given you the ok, the next step is setting a date to launch your book.

- **Rollout Your Marketing Campaign** – Now that your date is set, it is time to start marketing the upcoming release of your book.

Marketing Ideas

Create short YouTube videos about the topic of your book. You can provide the backstory, why you wrote the book etc. I recommend you upload them to Facebook as well.

Do a Google search for blogs that are related to your topic and contact the blog owner and ask if they would interview you on their blog. Make sure you provide them with a free digital proof copy of your book before the interview to show your appreciation.

Do a Google search for Online Radio Shows that are related to your topic and contact the show and ask if they would like to interview you. Make sure you provide them with a free digital proof copy of your book before the interview to show your appreciation.

Social Media – Change your Facebook cover to match your book, Tweet quotes from your book, post pics on Instagram. Share the process of anything related to the book, such as receiving your first copy, getting the cover designed etc.

Press Release – Write a press release or have one written for you and submit it online to every press outlet you can, especially your local press outlets (Newspaper, TV & Radio).

Plan A Book Signing – A great way to market the release of your new book is to set up a book signing at your local library or a public place that would let you have one.

Those are just a few ways you can market your book, there are a million more ways, just be creative.

- **Launch Book** – Finally the book is done, and it is time to launch the book! Make sure you are pushing the book hard on release day, stay active on social media, email family and friends, text family and friends and remind them to order a copy.

Keep Pushing – After your book has been launched continue pushing it, get as many interviews as you can, do as many book signings as you can and continue to share every step of the process. Share pictures of your book signings and news on social media.

Part 2 – Quick Start Guide To Getting Your Book Done Fast

In this section, I will share with you a simple method to getting your book done fast.

Step 1 - Get 15 Sheets of Paper

Step 2 – On page 1 write the title of the book.

Step 3 – On page 2 write the numbers 1-10 (See Example Below)

1. Chapter Title (Ex. Making Big Money with Books)
2. Chapter Title
3. Chapter Title
4. Chapter Title
5. Chapter Title
6. Chapter Title
7. Chapter Title
8. Chapter Title
9. Chapter Title
10. Chapter Title

Step 4 - On page 3 write the chapter title that you listed on page 2 as number 1 at the top. Then write 10 questions someone would have about that chapter title. (See Example Below)

Chapter Title - Making Big Money with Books
    Question 1 – How do you make big money with books?
    Question 2
    Question 3
    Question 4
    Question 5
    Question 6
    Question 7
    Question 8
    Question 9
    Question 10

Step 5- Complete the same task for pages 4-12, write the chapter title at the top. Then write 10 questions someone would have about that chapter title.
(See Example Below)

    Chapter Title – (Insert Second Chapter Title)
    Question 1
    Question 2
    Question 3
    Question 4
    Question 5
    Question 6
    Question 7
    Question 8
    Question 9
    Question 10

Step 6 – On page 13 write your Dedication & Acknowledgements

Step 7 – On page 14 write your bio

Step 8 – Write a list of any sources you may have included information from in your chapters.

Step 9 - Have someone interview you ask you the questions you listed under each chapter title.

Record the interview for free on Freeconferencing.com. They will send you an mp3 after the call is finished FREE of charge.

Step 10 - Have the audio from the interview transcribed.

Step 11 - Have transcribed document edited & formatted.

And Bam You Have a Book!

You can also record yourself answering the questions.

You can record with a free software called Audacity, you can get at (audacity.sourceforge.net)

After you are done recording yourself export recording as an mp3, then have the audio transcribed, then have the transcription edited & formatted.

Bonus Tip$$$

Have you done any public speaking or gave a lecture of any kind?

Record a video your lecture, then extract the audio, have it transcribed and turn it into a book!

Bonus Ideas

- Put on your own event and record yourself giving a lecture about your topic, then have it transcribed and turned into a book.
- Do a home presentation - Invite family and friends over to view your presentation, record yourself giving a lecture about your topic, then have it transcribed and turned into a book.
- Sunday School Lessons – Do you write and teach your own Sunday school lessons at church? Record yourself giving the lesson, and then have it transcribed and turned into a book.

Pastors / Preachers – Every Sunday when you give a sermon record it, then have it transcribed and turned into a book.

Here Is What You Need to Do Now

You need to release your first book!

Everybody has a book in them!

Becoming a Published Author Will Open Up So Many Doors / Opportunities You Probably Never Dreamed Of!

If you have ever wanted to be invited to speak at conferences or workshops, a book will put you in line as the expert!

Think about it, not only will you get an honorarium for speaking; you can go in the lobby and sell your books and put more spending cash in your pocket! Imagine that flight home with an extra $1,000 - $2,000 in your pocket!

I Know You Want More Money!

I Know You Want a Change in Your Life!

I Know You Want a Job where every day Is Payday?

I'm Going to Sell You on Things You Know You Should Be Doing…

I'm Going to Sell You on Taking the Actions You Know You Need to Take!

I'm Going to Sell You on A Whole New Life of Freedom!

Say These Three Words Below Out Loud!

TAKE ACTION NOW!

Because Tomorrow Never Comes...

What You Don't Do Today Doesn't Get Done!

What I'm about to share with you will change your life!

I'm going to Share with you our Book Publishing Package!

Before I Found My Passion...

I Worked Two Jobs 16-17-hour Days to Support My Family!

I Used To...

- Be afraid to lose that job I hated.
- Have to ask to go to my son's football and basketball games.
- Ask can I have a day off for my Anniversary, to take my wife to dinner.
- Get in trouble if I took too long on break!

I remember my last day at Wal-Mart, one of the managers looked at me and said: "You'll be just like the rest of them you'll be back!" I said, "No I won't!" I thank God because He has been Faithful!

Wal-Mart Does Not Control My Destiny Anymore!

I thank God, he has blessed me with an opportunity to help people's dreams come true, which was to become published authors!

This young lady is Jessie Rogers; she is 16 and was born blind. We made her dream of becoming a published author come to pass.

WOW, she is 16 & Born Blind and you're still making excuses?

Now when I started my business, I got invited on a conference call....

The guy on the call told me exactly what to do to make my dreams come true.

I Told Him, He Was Crazy!

Guess What?

I didn't **TAKE ACTION**…And It Cost Me At least $50,000!

Yes, I achieved some success, but had I taken action then on what he shared with me, my success would have come a lot faster!

When I Started to Take Action!
I Started Making Money!

Say the Words Below Out loud

Successful People Don't Ask How Much Something Costs, They Ask How Much Will It Make Me?

Question: How Do You Win at Monopoly?
Answer: YOU BUY EVERYTHING!

I Have a Book Publishing Package Called

Completely Turnkey!

Here Is What It Includes!

We will publish your book on Amazon & Amazon Kindle, Barnes & Noble, Books-A-Million & More!
We will complete your book formatting & editing.
We will provide you with a unique ISBN #.
We will provide a book cover design.
We will give physical copies of your book.
We will develop a complete marketing plan.
We will generate a book trailer/promo video to

complement your book and generate interest and sales.

Your book will print & ship on-demand, you won't have to touch a thing!

Complete Passive Income!

Plus, you will receive a link to order your book wholesale if you would like to have more physical copies to sell in person. As low as $2.15 per book!

Plus, you will maintain all rights to your work & 100% of your profits.

What If I Told You All You Had to Do Was Give Us Your Manuscript?

Your Publishing Package **Sets Up Everything for You!**

All You Have to Do Is Give Us Your Manuscript!

<u>The Publishing Package</u>

- We will Publish your book on Amazon & Amazon Kindle, Barnes & Noble, Books-A-Million & More!
- We will complete your book formatting & editing.
- We will provide you with a unique ISBN #.
- We will provide an eye-catching book cover.
- We will generate physical copies of your book.
- We will develop a complete marketing plan.
- We will generate a book trailer/promo video to complement your book and generate interest and sales.

- Books will print & ship on-demand.
- You can order your book wholesale.

You will maintain all rights to your work & 100% of your profits.

Your Publishing Package
Sets Up Everything for You!

All You Have to Do Is, Give Us Your Manuscript!

You Can Do THIS!

It's In You!

Here Is What You Need to Do; You Need to Get Signed Up for Our Publishing Package!

And Get Your Book Published!

It's Your Time to Hold Your Book in Your Hand!

Your Publishing Package
Sets Up Everything for You!

Get Started Now Visit:
www.PublishingAdvantageGroup.com
or Call 276-229-0530

There Comes a Point in Your Life When You Know You Need to Take a New Action.

There comes a point when the thing you need to do is so obvious...

Years from Now You're Going to Look Back at this Moment, you're going to say he gave me the Opportunity to Change my Life!

Get Started Now Visit:
www.PublishingAdvantageGroup.com
or Call 276-229-0530

ABOUT THE AUTHOR

Born in the most notorious housing project in the world "Cabrini Green" in Chicago, Illinois, Kelly Cole can literally say he came from nothing. Determined to not remain at the bottom, Kelly started his first business at age six with his sister. Kelly has owned two clothing stores, two restaurants and was a barber for ten years, all before finding his true passions: marketing and book publishing.

Kelly has since become the CEO of Publishing Advantage Group & Road Manager of Christian Recording Artist Aaron Cole, a 2X #1 Best Selling Author, Master Book Publisher, Coach, Entrepreneur, Speaker & Minister. Kelly has authored and published over 50+ paperback, audio and e-books to date.

Kelly has been seen on NBC, FOX, ABC, The CW, Gospel Updates Magazine & more. Kelly started Prime Time Marketing 12 years ago after quitting his day jobs at Wal-Mart & Blockbuster. He almost ended up homeless with his family, but worked hard serving and helping other people's dreams come true, which ultimately led to his dream coming true of building a successful marketing & book publishing company. In 2014, he was even inducted into the GrindMoves Hall of Fame.

He has been labeled A Business Guru for his knowledge and marketing wisdom that he has used to help people all over the world!

He is the proud father of three. He has one son & two daughters and has been married for over 16 years to his wife Natasha.

As a Coach and Consultant Kelly has worked with clients who have appeared on OWN, Real House Wives of ATL, Bravo, NBA, WORD network, MTV, BET, Atlantic Records, and more.

As an Entrepreneur & Marketing expert and panelist Kelly has spoken and appeared in numerous conferences, workshops, seminars, radio shows and publications.

Kelly believes you can have whatever you want out of life, "As long as you take the necessary action to get it!"

Kelly Cole is currently available for corporate, nonprofit, faith-based, and educational (middle/high school & college) speaking engagements, panel discussions, conferences, workshops or product consultation.

Highlights:

– 2X #1 Best Selling Author (Conversations with Sharks - Success Secrets Shared by The Sharks on ABC's Hit TV Show Shark Tank and Everyday Heroes)

– Inducted into the Grind Moves Hall of Fame in 2015

– Started First Business at Age 6

– Head of Guerilla marketing for the Christian Film "Believe" (Named 2016 Film of The Year – The Christian Film Review)

– Seen on NBC, FOX, ABC, The CW

– Appeared on the Cover Gospel Updates Magazine

– Authored and published over 50+ paperback, audio, and e-books to date.

– Judah Theological School of Ministry (Course Instructor)

– eBay Power-seller

– Co-Creator of Write Your Way Out Now Writer's Conference

– Norfolk State University – Entrepreneurship Fall Speaker (2X)

– Northwest Mississippi Community College (Speaker)

– Optimist Club (Speaker)

– Talk About It Today with Mo Stegall Radio Show ATL ~ Weekly Marketing Moment Host

– How to Make Money, Money, Money Online Internet Work Shop (Speaker/ Presenter) (6X) Atlanta, GA

– Make Dot Com Dollars Internet Work (Speaker) Chicago, IL

– Chetwyn Rodgers Development Center Small Biz Workshop (Speaker) Chicago, IL

Visit: www.MrKellyCole.com
For More Of Kelly Products & Services

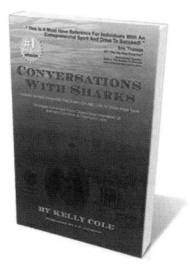

Made in the USA
Columbia, SC
17 January 2018